FCE Result

Writing & Speaking Assessment Booklet

Petrina Cliff

OXFORD
UNIVERSITY PRESS

Great Clarendon Street, Oxford OX2 6DP

Oxford University Press is a department of the University of Oxford.
It furthers the University's objective of excellence in research, scholarship,
and education by publishing worldwide in

Oxford New York

Auckland Cape Town Dar es Salaam Hong Kong Karachi
Kuala Lumpur Madrid Melbourne Mexico City Nairobi
New Delhi Shanghai Taipei Toronto

With offices in

Argentina Austria Brazil Chile Czech Republic France Greece
Guatemala Hungary Italy Japan Poland Portugal Singapore
South Korea Switzerland Thailand Turkey Ukraine Vietnam

OXFORD and OXFORD ENGLISH are registered trade marks of
Oxford University Press in the UK and in certain other countries

ISBN: 978 0 19 480060 0

Printed in China

ACKNOWLEDGEMENTS

*The publisher would like to thank the following for their kind permission to reproduce
photographs*: Alamy pp 28 (corridor/Hanan Isachar), (family on bike/Alex
Segre), 29 (school teacher/Greenhills), 30 (palm pool), (sunset/Pictures),
(family meal/FAN travelstock), 31 (hotel exterior/Stan Rohrer); Corbis Images
p 31 (palm trees/Bob Krist), (archaeological guide/Dave G Houser); Jumeirah
International Hotels p 30 (hotel room); Zooid Pictures p 29 (ski class).

The authors and publisher would like to thank: the students of Eckersley School
of English, Oxford and International House, Bath. *Notes and assessment by:*
Margaret Matthews and Caroline Antonyuk.

Contents

Assessing Writing

Introduction   4

Assessment Criteria for Writing   5

Authentic written answers   6

Assessing Speaking

Introduction   18

Assessment Criteria for Speaking   20

Paper 5 Worksheets   21

Giving a good performance   26

Examiner's questions   27

Paper 5 photos   28

Answer key   32

Introduction to Assessing Writing

In Paper 2 Writing, candidates are required to answer two questions from two parts. The first part consists of a compulsory question; the second part consists of four questions from which candidates must select one.

In Part 1 candidates are asked to write either a letter or an email. They will have to read up to 160 words of input information; this could be an advertisement, an extract from a letter or something similar. Candidates use this information to answer the task and write an answer in 120–150 words.

In Part 2, candidates' answers should be 120–180 words. The possible tasks are:

Article – often written for an English-language publication. Students should write an interesting and engaging article on a given topic. They will need to describe something and perhaps give opinions.

Email – written to a friend or a tutor and answering a task provided. Even though this is an email, candidates should still use properly formed grammatical sentences and accurate spelling.

Essay – written for a teacher, possibly including opinions or ideas on a subject outlined in the task.

Letter – candidates write a reply to a given situation, such as applying for a job or course. They will need to choose from a wide range of functions such as requesting information or making suggestions.

Report – could be written for a teacher/principal or other students. It should be clearly organised with factual information and involve functions such as making recommendations.

Review – like the article, written for an English language publication. Candidates should describe a given topic and give their personal opinion.

Short story – often written for an English language publication and requiring an organised and creative answer that engages the reader.

Set text – task types include articles, essays, letters, reports and reviews.

Assessment Criteria for Writing

Answers are assessed on the fulfilment of the task and also given a general impression mark. Candidates need to read the task very carefully and make sure they address each part within it. For example, if candidates are asked to write a letter suggesting a time and place to meet, but their answer only suggests a place, then the task is not complete. This would prevent the student achieving a better mark, however good the language and the structure of the answer may be. The general impression refers to the candidate's ability to write in a suitable register (formal or informal) for the intended reader, the organisation and structure of the answer, and the range of vocabulary and grammatical structures used.

There are six bands, ranging from Band 0 (the lowest) to Band 5 (the highest).

Band 5 fully achieves the desired effect on the reader. All points of the task are addressed and expanded, ideas effectively organised, with well-developed language, minimal errors, and register consistently appropriate.

Band 4 achieves the desired effect on the reader. All points of the task are included, ideas clearly organised, with generally accurate language, some errors, and register appropriate on the whole.

Band 3 on the whole achieves the desired effect on the reader. All points of the task are included, ideas adequately organised, with adequate range of language, a number of errors, and a reasonable attempt (though not always successful) at register.

Band 2 does not have the desired effect on the reader. Some points of the task are missing or poorly covered and/or irrelevant points added, ideas are inadequately organised, with a limited range of language, errors which distract the reader, and unsuccessful or inconsistent use of register.

Band 1 has a very negative effect on the reader. There are notable omissions of points in the task, possibly due to misinterpretation of the task. There is a lack of organisation, a narrow range of language, frequent errors, and little awareness of register.

Band 0 would be given to an incomplete, irrelevant or illegible answer.

Assessed written answers

On pages 6 to 17 of this booklet there are 12 authentic answers to the questions in the Writing sections of *FCE Result* Student's Book. These appear exactly as written by real students, with assessment based on the Assessment Criteria above. These can be used by teachers as a guide to marking their own students' work. They are also photocopiable so that they could, if teachers wish, be used in class to show examples of other students' answers to the tasks in *FCE Result* Student's Book. The assessment should act as a reminder to students of what the task requirements are and how they can successfully answer the questions. The models can be used as a basis for discussion, for example, what features of them are particularly good or weak, and what improvements could be made.

Unit 1 (p18) An informal letter

Notes

Content
The informal letter should describe the writer's plans for the summer.

Organisation and cohesion
Clear organisation and paragraphing, with use of linking words where appropriate.

Appropriacy of register and format
Neutral or informal.

Range
Describing plans (the main function), and other functions such as expressing opinions or giving reasons, as appropriate.

Target reader
Friend.

Dear Chloe

Hi. How are you?

I've just received your E-mail.

Now I'm very exciting because of my summer holidays.

I decided to go the Fiji. Now I'm looking for my accomodation and flight.

You know, I've never had holiday since I started my own business. So I need to take a rest.

I'm going there with my family for 2 weeks.

I'd like to learn scuba diving and swimming there Actually, I'm afraid to do something in the sea. But I'll try. It would be very fun.

Of course most of my time will be on the beach to sunbathing.

These days weather in my town is awful. I've never seen sunshine for a long time.

If you go to Fiji with us, it will be good.

How about going with us? I wish you will be with us

By the way, How's your husband?

I heard that he had a car accident. Is he alright?

Say hello to him.

Please answer me as soon as you possible.

Best wishes

Jiyeon

Assessment

This answer would probably achieve a Band 3 score.

Content
The task is completed adequately. The final part of the letter (enquiry about husband's accident) falls outside the scope of the task, and at 168 words this final part would be excluded from assessment. The details given by the writer about his/her plans include reasons for taking a holiday, the types of activity he/she is hoping to do, and his/her feelings about the prospect of the holiday. They are relevant and varied, and would be of interest to the recipient.

Accuracy
There are minor mistakes in most sentences, but none which impede understanding.

Range
Adequate range of vocabulary and structures.

Organisation and cohesion
The sequencing of ideas is quite loose: information is not always arranged in a coherent way. There are many short paragraphs, some of which are only the length of a single sentence and the divisions are not always appropriate. For example, the sentence about sunbathing is separated from the sentence about the weather, and it would have been appropriate to link these two ideas.

Awareness of audience
Appropriate to the task. Good use of informal language.

Target reader
Would be informed.

Unit 2 (p30) A formal email

Notes

Content
The email should request details of the wildlife expedition: which animals will be studied, where and when the induction course takes place. The email should also give details of the writer's proficiency in Spanish and swimming.

Organisation and cohesion
Clear organisation and paragraphing, with use of linking words where appropriate.

Appropriacy of register and format
Formal.

Range
Requesting information, giving information, describing personal skills and abilities.

Target Reader
Company representative.

Dear Sir or Madam,

I'm writing to volunteer to take part in the conservation expedition to Costa Rica. My reason for volunteering is that I'd like to broaden my experience as a biologist. Indeed, I obtained my degree 3 months ago.

The advertisement says you will be researching wildlife in the rainforest and in the waters. I'd be pleased if you could send me further information about where the research in water will be taking place and what kind of species you will be studying.

Furthermore, I'd be grateful if you could inform me if volunteers should take a specific physical test or if a diploma is required. Genarally speaking, I'd like to say I'm in good shape and an expert swimmer.

With reference to the request that some knowledge of Spanish is desirable, I'd like to mention that I'm a native Spanish speaker.

Fimally, if I'm lucky enough in case I will be selected for joining the expedition, I'd be glad if you could give some details about where and when the two-week induction course will take place.

Thanking you all in advance.

I look forward to hearing from you.

Yours faithfully,

Maria

Assessment

This answer would probably achieve a Band 5 score.

Content
The task is completed with full expansion of the content points. Plenty of detail is given and the language is rich and varied. Register is consistently appropriate throughout. One content point is addressed in a slightly different manner from that required by the task: the candidate has said that she is a native speaker of Spanish, where the task rubric states 'Basic Spanish. Give details'. This might prevent the candidate from receiving top marks.

Accuracy
The candidate displays very good control of language and errors are minimal. Errors tend to be limited to prepositions and word order is occasionally faulty.

Range
A wide range of structures and vocabulary is used appropriately and skilfully.

Organisation and cohesion
The writing is well organised. Paragraphing is used to good effect with a new paragraph for each point made. Cohesive devices, including reference and substitution are used throughout.

Awareness of audience
Appropriate to the task. Good use of formal language.

Target reader
Would be fully informed.

Unit 3 (p42) A story

Notes

Content
The story should describe events which were amusing or unusual, and which happened in one of the following contexts:
- a school lesson
- a social outing
- a shopping trip

Organisation and cohesion
Clear organisation and paragraphing, with use of linking words where appropriate.

Appropriacy of register and format
Any style would be suitable, providing it is used consistently.

Range
Describing past events (the main function), and other functions such as describing people and places or expressing opinions, as appropriate.

Target reader
Teacher.

A funny thing happened when I was out with my friend. I was not normal evening. We spent a time in without anyone men! This was the last weekend before my closed friend weding. We started that evening in my home. Some of girls bring presents for my friend. Most of them where jokes. She was ashamed because she was forced to wear strange clothes. As a result she took it on her clothes. Then we went out to the pub. We started the special game. Each girls could let my friend do something weird or funny. At the begining things were simple. Future bride had to jump on her one leg round the table. She also had to dance on the bar. Later we let her find ten people, actually men and tell them how much she loves her partner. Some of them where completely suprised. I find it hard to just come and say "hello I am Ana I would like to tell you something". There was a lot of laugh and we had great fun. Finally we change the local once more and went dancing in the night club. I remember that evening as one of funniest in my life. In my opinion we should not have forgotten about this nice custom.

Assessment

This answer would probably achieve a Band 2 score.

Content
The requirements of the task are fully met. However, the story is well over length, and the writer could have spent less time writing and more time checking (see Accuracy below).

The writer narrates the events of the evening, and intersperses facts with comment and opinion. He/she clearly expresses the amusing aspects of the evening, as required.

Accuracy
Mistakes in grammar and spelling are frequent, and unfortunately these sometimes delay or obstruct understanding.

Range
An adequate range of vocabulary is used. Few complex grammatical structures are attempted.

Organisation and cohesion
The writer narrates the events of the evening in a clear sequence. He/she also uses linking words such as 'Then', 'Later', and 'Finally' to good effect, and these, together with accurate pronoun use, help the reader to follow the outline of the story without effort. However, there are no paragraph divisions.

Awareness of audience
The style is appropriate to the task.

Target reader
Would be fully informed.

Unit 4 (p54) A review

Notes

Content
The review should give information about a film. It may include references to actors/actresses, setting, storyline etc, and should include an evaluation of the film.

Organisation and cohesion
Clear organisation and paragraphing, with use of linking words where appropriate.

Appropriacy of register and format
Moderately informal, neutral or formal style, used consistently.

Range
Describing people, places and/or events; expressing opinions; giving reasons.

Target reader
Readers of film magazine.

Pride and Prejudice

First of all, I have to say that this movie is very romantic so if you are not interested in love stories forget it. Nevertheless, for those people who love romantic scenery and lovely landscape at the background they should definitely see this movie.

In my opinion Pride and Prejudice has everything what you can expect from a good made film. The plot is really exciting, the figures are great acted and the music makes it sensitive and full of love. From my point of view it is always very difficult to make a movie based on a book story, especially when it is written by such a known writer as Jane Austin is. However, in this case it has been made a really good work.

I am not going to tell you all the story, it will be pointless but the only thing I can tell you is this: you can suspect a typical love story which is made in a very very special way.

What can I add?! Just enjoy it! I am sure that you will definitely like it.

Assessment

This answer would probably achieve a Band 4 score.

Content
The task is fully completed and reaches the upper limit of the required length. The writer refers to various aspects of the film, including plot, acting, music and scenery, and supports his/her opinions with reasons. His/her enthusiasm for the film is clearly conveyed.

Accuracy
There are some grammatical and vocabulary mistakes, but these do not obstruct understanding.

Range
An adequate range of both vocabulary and structures is used.

Organisation and cohesion
Ideas are quite clearly organised, moving from the general content of the film, through details of the production, to an overall evaluation. Paragraph divisions are clearly marked, and linking expressions such as 'First of all' and 'In my opinion' are used appropriately.

Awareness of audience
The style is appropriate to the task.

Target reader
Would be informed and engaged.

Unit 5 (p66) An essay

Notes

Content
The essay should express an opinion about the question posed in the task, and give reasons for the opinion.

Organisation and cohesion
Clear organisation and paragraphing, with use of linking words where appropriate.

Appropriacy of register and format
Neutral or formal.

Range
Expressing and justifying opinions (main functions), and other functions such as giving examples as appropriate.

Target reader
Teacher.

I think that to be honest isn't the best way everytime. You mustn't be honest with your friends to tell them that he looks today very bad.

The doctors mustn't be honest with deathly-ill patients.

They have to be honest with their family.

There are lots of things you have to be honest to. This is also a question of education.

Whatever, you have to be honest with you, with your family, work, friends, your life.

...with your self.

To 'be able to look' in the mirror and known you haven't ever done something what could hurt somebody else.

Assessment

This answer would probably achieve a Band 2 score.

Content
This essay is under length, and the content is rather thin. Although the writer does address the question, and remain focused, his/her opinion is not well supported. He/she describes various situations which require, or don't require honesty, but it is only the last sentence which provides any justification for the writer's opinion.

Accuracy
There are several inaccuracies of grammar but these never obstruct understanding, and the vocabulary used is mainly correct.

Range
More complex grammatical structures are not attempted, and the range of vocabulary used is fairly narrow.

Organisation and cohesion
The logic of the writer's essay is easy to follow: first he/she describes situations where honesty is not the best policy, then situations where it is, and finally he/she suggests a guiding principle. The shortness of the essay means that paragraph divisions are generally poor. For example, it isn't clear how the third and fourth paragraphs relate to each other, and why they are separate.

The essay suffers from an almost complete lack of linking words and this means the writer cannot demonstrate how the topics of the various sentences and paragraphs are connected.

Awareness of audience
The style used is appropriate for the readership of an essay.

Target reader
Would be partially informed.

Unit 6 (p78) An informal email

Notes

Content
The email should contain all the points in the notes:
- describe the best way to get from the airport to the house at about 5pm
- suggest some local places to visit
- explain the writer's lack of free time during friend's visit
- identify local galleries and/or museums (not necessary to give details)

Organisation and cohesion
Clear organisation and paragraphing, with use of linking words where appropriate.

Appropriacy of register and format
Informal or neutral; standard grammar and spelling.

Range
Expressing pleasure, giving information, making suggestions, expressing regret, explaining.

Target reader
Friend.

Hi Paula

Long time no see! I'm looking forward to seeing you. I saw your mail yesterday. Coul you call me as soon as you arrive. I think I might be in school when you call me I will go to home for you.

Anyway. You take a airplane remousine in front of airport. It is not expensive and easy way to get to my home. You should get off the Su-Yu station which is near my home and then call me. I'll pick you up. It is just 5 minutes on foot, I'm afraid I don't have much time to visit Seoul with you. but I might stay with you just for 2 days. because I'm taking mid-term exam unfortunately.

I recomend some good places to visit by yourself. Insadary is a traditional street. There are a lot of traditional Korean artworks and traditional gallery. It is my favorite street. It is not far from my house and easy to get to there. You just take No. 150 bus. If you have enough to visit another place How about going to Kyangbokgung. As you know, we have long history. Kyangbokgung is a kind of palace such as Buckingham Place. Seoul has been being capital of South Korea for 600 years. but I'm afraid we don't have a lot of historical instructure because of Korean War.

Fortunately, we have some museums. National museum is good for you. I think you have to spend much time there because there are a lot of artworks, memorials and paintings. It is centre of Seoul so It's not difficult to find this you just take a subway

I want you to enjoy visiting seoul. I'm waiting you.

Your best friend

Mingu

Assessment
This answer would probably achieve a Band 4 score.

Content
All required points are covered and suitably expanded, and there are no irrelevant digressions. The writer has provided factual information as well as appropriate comment. However, the email is considerably over the required length, so some of the time spent writing could have been saved for checking.

Accuracy
There is a small proportion of grammatical, spelling and punctuation mistakes, but these rarely obstruct comprehension.

Range
A wide range of vocabulary and structures are used.

Organisation and cohesion
The content is organised clearly, as the email moves from one point to the next in an orderly way. The writer uses separate paragraphs for each of the points covered and this guides the reader through the email.

The use of pronouns also helps the email to flow, but there is a general shortage of linking words, which would have helped in this respect too.

Awareness of audience
Very appropriate to the task. There is good use of colloquial expressions and informal vocabulary.

Target reader
The reader would be fully informed, and react positively to the tone.

Unit 7 (p90) An informal email

Notes

Content
The informal email should contain all the points in the notes:

- say how the writer remembers his/her friend
- describe main events in writer's life since seeing friend
- agree to meeting and suggest time and place
- enquire about friend's news

Organisation and cohesion
Clear organisation and paragraphing, with use of linking words where appropriate.

Appropriacy of register and format
Informal or neutral; standard grammar and spelling.

Range
Expressing surprise/pleasure; giving information; making suggestions; asking for information.

Target reader
Friend.

Dear Liz.

Hi, How are you?

Of course, I remember you! I miss you!

Why didn't you tell me about your leaving? I was very sad when I realized you were leaving.

I'm a university student. How about you? Probably you are a student as well, right?

Now, I'm in France to study French for a year. But it is going to finish. so I'm going to there tomorrow. It means I can meet you! How lucky!

I'd like to meet you very much and as soon as possible. Where do you live now? Why couldn't we meet each other. in such as a small country!

Do you like Britney Spears still? I can remember that you were big fan of her. Is it right? And you used to go to swimming pool. All the time you asked me to go there. but I was afraid of water, so I couldn't go with you. Now I can swim so we can go together. I'd like to talk with you all about our old memory. right now!

By the way What have you been doing since we last met?

I'm wondering about that.

And where shall we mee? In front of the our school?

Please write and tell me

Best wishes

Jiyeon

Assessment

This answer would probably achieve a Band 3 score.

Content
Three of the content points are covered, but there is no suggestion for a time to meet, which was one of the required points. On the other hand, the writer appears to digress at times from the main agenda. For example, references to Britney Spears and swimming are not relevant.

The email is over the required length, so some of the time spent writing could have been saved for checking or careful planning.

Accuracy
There is a small proportion of grammatical, spelling and punctuation mistakes, but these only obstruct comprehension once or twice.

Range
A good range of vocabulary and grammatical structures are used.

Organisation and cohesion
Linking words are used appropriately, but the email is poorly organised: it lacks a clear overall sequence and repeats topics. For example, the meeting is referred to in the middle of the email, and then again at the end.

Paragraphing is used to fairly good effect, but sometimes the divisions do not seem to be in the most helpful places. For example, the final three or four sentences could be joined.

Awareness of audience
Very appropriate to the task. There is good use of colloquial expressions and informal vocabulary.

Target reader
Would be mainly informed, and would probably react positively to the tone.

Unit 8 (p102) A report

Notes

Content
The report should describe the advantages and disadvantages of the specific suggestions, and give reasons for the opinions expressed.

Organisation and cohesion
Clear organisation and paragraphing, with use of linking words where appropriate.

Appropriacy of register and format
Neutral or formal.

Range
Describing advantages and disadvantages (main function), and other functions such as giving reasons and examples as appropriate.

Target reader
Director of language school.

The director's proposal of to close the canteen and re-design in that place a student recreation room is quite controversial. Further down I will try to show the benefits and the drawbacks of this proposal.

At the first, the advantages are the students would be able to meet themself, they would be happy to have a new space for them, also this space would be a good oportunite to develop the speak skills.

On the other hand, If the canteen has been closed the people won't be a place to buy a food and maybe enjoy with other kind of people.

That's the reason I believe the director should be put the advantages and disadvantage on the weigh and decide about the best way to follow.

Assessment

This answer would probably achieve a Band 2 score.

Content
The writer's response to the task, though it meets the minimum length requirement, is rather thin. The first and fourth paragraphs do little more than re-state the task itself, so only half of the report deals with the substance of the task. In addition, the second paragraph refers to 'a new space', whereas the task refers to a change of use, so the advantages the writer describes (meeting and speaking) are not appropriate.

Accuracy
Vocabulary is largely accurate, but there are several inaccuracies of grammar which slow down understanding.

Range
The writer sometimes uses complex grammatical structures with a degree of success. The range of vocabulary is fairly narrow.

Organisation and cohesion
The logic of the writer's essay is easy to follow, and is clearly reflected by the paragraph divisions: first an introduction, then a description of the advantages of the proposals, then the disadvantages, and finally a conclusion.

A good attempt is made to use linking words, which underline the flow between ideas.

Awareness of audience
The style used is appropriate for the readership of an essay.

Target reader
Would be partially informed.

Unit 9 (p114) A letter

Notes

Content
The letter should ask for information regarding:

- where the accommodation is situated
- whether places are available between 12–13 August
- whether the stated cost includes meals and equipment hire
- what the lower age limit is

Organisation and cohesion
Clear organisation and paragraphing, with use of linking words where appropriate.

Appropriacy of register and format
Neutral or formal.

Range
Asking for information (main functions), and other functions such as giving information or expressing preferences, as appropriate.

Target reader
Company representative.

Dear Adrenalin adventure

I read your advertisement in the adventure magazine last month.

It has the advertisement for having two days adventure holidays with kayaking, hill-walking, surfing, wind-surfing mountain-biking, climbing, horse-riding.

We are a group of 6 people and we would like to go on the 12–13/8. Are there any places available for this days?

And what about the cost?

The £199, are there meals and hire of equipment included?

The last question I have is about the age.

One girl in our group is only 17. And you welcome only adults.

Is it possible to take her with us?

That's it.

Waiting for your answer.

Kind regards.

Assessment

This answer would probably achieve a Band 3 score.

Content
The letter is slightly under the minimum length, and the section about the activities on offer has been copied from the advertisement, and is redundant. Three points are covered, but one (the question about the location of the cabins) has been omitted.

Accuracy
Grammar is largely accurate, and the few errors which do appear do not affect understanding. Vocabulary is also accurate.

Range
Most of the words and structures the writer uses appear in the advertisement itself, so there is little evidence that the writer can access a wider range of these.

Organisation and cohesion
The letter moves from one point to another without repetition or overlap, and in this respect it is easy to follow. However, there are few linking words (apart from 'The last question I have...') to help the reader establish the link between topics, and paragraph divisions are unclear too. On the other hand, the writer's question about the minimum age limit, which is clearly separated from other topics, is inappropriately presented over two separate paragraphs.

Awareness of audience
The style used is inconsistent at times, for example the use of 'That's it' to signal closure is too informal for this type of letter.

Target reader
Would be mainly informed.

Unit 10 (p126) A letter

Notes

Content
The letter of application should ask for information regarding:

- the type of course preferred
- the subject preferred
- English language ability and qualifications
- reasons for wanting to study at this university

Organisation and cohesion
Clear organisation and paragraphing, with use of linking words where appropriate.

Appropriacy of register and format
Neutral or formal.

Range
Expressing preferences, giving information, explaining (main functions), and other functions such as describing ability and achievements, as appropriate.

Target reader
Director of Studies at a language school.

Dear. Martin Jarvis

I've read your advertisment at the newspaper. I'd like to study in the part-time course in English for FCE in your University.

I'm 21 year-old and my subject is French literature. I'm studying in Oxford for English language course at the moment. It'll be finished in December.

I wish to study there, I'd like to get the certification of FCE. Because of seeking my job. These days lots of company require a FCE result so I'd like to get it.

I hope your answer as soon as possible.

Yours sincerely,

Assessment

This answer would probably achieve a Band 2 score.

Content
This letter is below the minimum length required, although all the points are covered. The section about language abilities and qualifications could have been expanded, for example by details about employment or opportunities for practice.

Accuracy
There are several inaccuracies of grammar but these never obstruct understanding, and the vocabulary used is mainly correct.

Range
On the whole, only simple structures are attempted, and there are too many short sentences. The range of vocabulary used is adequate.

Organisation and cohesion
The writer organised his/her ideas in a very clear sequence, and paragraph divisions are both obvious and appropriate. The structure would have been further improved with the use of one or two appropriate linking words. Two unclear pronouns – 'there' and 'it' in the third paragraph – cause temporary problems for the reader.

Awareness of audience
The style used is completely appropriate for a letter of application.

Target reader
Would be mainly informed.

Unit 11 (p138) A letter of complaint

Notes

Content
The letter should describe the problems the candidate had with the mobile phone and the company's customer service.

Organisation and cohesion
Clear organisation and paragraphing, with use of linking words where appropriate.

Appropriacy of register and format
Formal.

Range
Describing problems, complaining, asking for a refund.

Target Reader
Company representative.

Dear Sir

I'm writting to ask the refund about my new mobile phone which I ordered on the internet, because there are sueral drawbacks.

Firstly, I ordered Mobifone 612 and asked to deliver no later than 1 Oct 2007, but I could receive one box 2 days later and the model was also wrong model "Mobifone 1100". As the result, I couldn't use my new mobile phone during my business trip which is supposed to do.

Secondly, I searched the other internet shopping mall yesterday. And I found the same model 'Mobifone 612' was being sold in cheaper price. So your advertisement "unbeatable prices" says the wrong information about the price. With this reason, I'd like to refund my payment by your terms & conditions.

Thirdly, the wrongly delivered mobile phone is more expensive than original one. 100 pounds was overcharged me.

By the above reasons, I'd like to inform you that I was very unsatisfied about you services and mistakes and ask to refund the payment. It would be appreciate if you take suitable steps as soon as possible.

Sincerely

SM Lee

Assessment

This answer would probably achieve a Band 3 score.

Content
The task is completed with relevant expansion of the content points. The details given are relevant and varied and register is consistently appropriate.

Accuracy
Control of language is average and errors occur where more complex language is attempted. These mistakes impede communication in places. The message is relatively clear.

Range
A fair range of structures is used and there is a wide range of relevant vocabulary, used with some skill and flexibility.

Organisation and cohesion
The writing is well organised and paragraphing is relevant and clear with a new paragraph for each point made. Cohesive devices are used appropriately but with limited flexibility.

Awareness of audience
Appropriate to the task. Good use of formal language.

Target reader
Would be fully informed.

Unit 12 (p150) An article

Notes

Content
The article should make three suggestions for changes which would improve the local environment.

Organisation and cohesion
Clear organisation and paragraphing, with use of linking words where appropriate.

Appropriacy of register and format
Any style would be suitable, provided it is used consistently.

Range
Expressing opinions (main function); other supporting functions such as explaining, or describing places/ activities as appropriate.

Target reader
Readers of magazine about environmental issues.

If you want to improve enviroment in your town or village.

You have to change a lot of thinking and activity about enviroment. Therefore, I will sugget three solution in my essay.

Firstly, we need to change developing systems because Nowdays a lot of apartment, house and public buildings are made by people. If someone want to build some buildings, they must affect enviroment. For instance, cut many trees, demolish old buildings and crash the mountain. It will remain a lot of rubbish and various pollution in the world. Therefore, we should limit build buildings.

Secondly, we have to recycle many things like foods and plastic. Specially, we sperate food trash from other things because it rots very fast and it create various insects like flies and mosquitos then it affects harmful to people. In addition, if some food rubbish mix other things then we cannot recycle it.

Thirdly, a lot of people change thinking about environment. because I suppose that you have bad thinking about it then you do not keep the enviroment. For example, you will throw rubbishes everywhere then younger people copy you.

In conclusion, we must protect enviroment. Therefore, we basictely change small things!

Assessment
This answer would probably achieve a Band 3 score.

Content
All three points are clearly made, and suitably supported with reasons. However, the writer makes no reference to the local context (his/her own town or village), and seems to refer instead to general issues concerning the environment. Therefore the task is not fully addressed.

Accuracy
Spelling and vocabulary are generally accurate, but mistakes of grammar and punctuation are frequent. Structural errors frequently delay or obstruct understanding.

Range
The range of vocabulary is adequate. Complex structures are attempted, but lack accuracy.

Organisation and cohesion
The article is very clearly organised: there is an introduction, a conclusion, and three specific suggestions for change, all clearly divided into separate paragraphs, and introduced by suitable linking words ('Firstly', 'In conclusion' etc). The reader is threefore given maximum help to follow the development of the article.

Awareness of audience
A suitable style is used throughout.

Target reader
Would be partially informed.

Introduction to Assessing Speaking

How to use the DVD and worksheets

FCE Result Teacher's DVD and this accompanying section in the Assessment Booklet are designed to familiarise teachers and students with the format and requirements of Paper 5 Speaking. The material can be used alongside *FCE Result* but since it is not intrinsically tied to the course, it will make a useful complement to any course at this level.

Although the DVD does not show any actual exam footage, the formats of the tests are scripted according to Cambridge guidelines, the 'candidates' are real students studying for the FCE exam in Oxford, and the 'examiners' are experienced oral examiners. Different students and combinations of students are shown doing different parts of the test, except in the complete test, which features the same two students throughout. Teachers should make it clear to their students that they will do the whole test with just one other candidate, or occasionally, where there is an odd number of students at the end of an examining session, with two other candidates.

The DVD can be used at any point in the course for training, and will make a useful revision tool. It is recommended that teachers watch all of the DVD before showing all or part of it to their students. They can then choose to show their students all of the DVD, or individual sections, most of which are accompanied by a Worksheet. Recommendations are given as to which sections students should watch before doing the Worksheets, but this is flexible according to different teaching situations and students' needs. The Worksheets and other suggested activities can be done individually or in small groups as appropriate.

FCE Result Teacher's DVD contains the following:

Overview of the Speaking Test and explanation of the **format** of the four Parts of the test, each one followed by an example of different students carrying out the relevant tasks.

Explanation of the **Assessment Criteria** used by the examiners. A summary of these can also be found on page 20 of this booklet.

Advice on how candidates can **give a good performance** in each part of the test, including examples of typical errors and tips on how to do well. Each Part is followed by an example of different students carrying out the tasks. Some examples show students making typical errors, others show students giving a good performance, according to the advice summarised by the examiner.

A **complete test** showing two students carrying out an uninterrupted test. This is followed by a **general assessment** of their performance according to the Assessment Criteria.

The photocopiable Worksheets on pages 21 to 27 can be used in class as follows:

Worksheet 1 (page 21)
This focuses on the format of each Part of the test and the role of the examiners. Students will be able to do this Worksheet after watching the **Overview** section of the DVD.

Worksheets 2 to 5 (pages 22 to 25) are based on the examples of students doing each part of the test in the **Overview** section. The tasks focus on their performance according to the task requirements and Assessment Criteria. It is recommended that students watch at least the whole of the **Overview** section before doing these Worksheets.

A summary of the advice given for each part in **Giving a good performance** can be found on page 26, along with some useful phrases. Students can refer to these before practising the test themselves. The photos used are reproduced on pages 28 to 31, and are photocopiable for use in class. Students could take turns to role play candidates and examiners. The transcript of the **examiner's questions** from the DVD is on page 27. It is recommended that students watch the complete test as a model before practising this themselves, although some teachers may prefer to get students to try the test first then watch the example before practising again.

The answer key for the Worksheets is on page 32.

Other possible activities

1 Show students the **Giving a good performance** section, and at the end of each example check that they have understood whether the 'candidates' on the DVD have followed the advice or not. The key on page 32 confirms what each student shown in this section has done right or wrong.

2 Show students the whole DVD including the complete test, but not the examiner's assessment. Ask students to say how well they think the 'candidates' did in each part according to the Assessment Criteria. This could be done as a whole class or discussed in small groups before feeding back. Students then watch the examiner's assessment to compare their answers.

Changes to Paper 5 Speaking from December 2008

• The timing and format of this Paper remain the same.

• In Part 2 candidates are no longer asked to 'compare and contrast' their pictures, but just to 'compare' them and answer a question or questions about them. These will appear as prompts on the picture sheet.

• In Part 3 the examiner's questions will also appear as prompts on the picture sheet.

Assessment Criteria for Speaking

Candidates are assessed throughout the test by two examiners, the Interlocutor and the Assessor. The assessment is based on candidates' performance over the whole test. The Assessor gives marks for:

- Grammar and Vocabulary
- Discourse Management
- Pronunciation
- Interactive Communication.

The Interlocutor gives a mark for Global Achievement.

Grammar and Vocabulary

Candidates are marked on their ability to use grammar accurately and appropriately, and a range of vocabulary suitable to the tasks.

Discourse Management

Candidates should be able to talk without too much hesitation, and to organise what they say into coherent speech.

Pronunciation

Candidates are marked on their ability to pronounce individual sounds with correct stress and intonation; the examiners assess the overall effect of candidates' pronunciation and the amount of effort needed to understand what they say.

Interactive Communication

Candidates are marked on how well they take part in the conversation and develop the discussion by asking and responding to questions appropriately.

Global Achievement

The Interlocutor gives an independent impression mark for the candidates' overall ability to carry out the tasks in each Part of the test.

Worksheet 1

Overview

1 There are usually .... candidates taking the test together.

2 There are a .... of examiners.

3 The Assessor listens and gives a .... assessment.

4 The test lasts for approximately .... minutes.

5 At the end of the test the examiners .... the candidates for ....

Part 1

6 Candidates talk about themselves and give information about their ....

7 Candidates are generally asked questions in ....

Part 2

8 Candidates need to talk for a full ....

9 They are shown .... colour photographs.

10 Candidates have to .... the photographs then answer another question.

11 The questions are also written on ....

Part 3

12 Candidates discuss something together for about .... minutes.

13 They are given a sheet with .... pictures.

14 The examiner's prompts appear on the sheet in the form of two ....

Part 4

15 The questions in this part are related to the discussion in ....

16 Unlike in Part 1, the questions are not personal, but are more .... based.

Worksheet 2

Part 1

Maximiliane and Maxim

1 After the Interlocutor has introduced himself and the Assessor, what is the first question he asks the candidates?

....

2 **a** What does the Interlocutor ask Maximiliane and Maxim to give him?

....

   b What does he do with them?

....

3 Do Maximiliane and Maxim give full answers to the questions in this Part?

....

4 When Maximiliane is asked to tell the examiners about her family, which of these does she mention?

- How many brothers and sisters she has. ☐

- How old they are. ☐

- Where she lives at the moment. ☐

- What her parents do for a living. ☐

5 The Interlocutor asks Maxim 'Is there anything new you'd really like to learn about?'. Does Maxim give a reason for his answer?

....

6 What answer would you give to the question in 5?

....

Worksheet 3

Part 2

Melanie and Costanza

1 Before she shows the candidates their photos, what does the Interlocutor do?

....

2 Does the Interlocutor give Melanie and Costanza their photos at the same time?

....

3 Does Melanie spend time thinking before she starts talking about her photos?

....

4 Is what Melanie does in question 3 the correct thing to do?

....

5 Does Melanie compare the photos and answer the question?

....

6 Does Melanie speak for a full minute?

....

7 Who do you think gives a better answer to their follow-up question about their partner's photos? Why?

....

8 Costanza's follow-up question is 'Do you enjoy cycling?'.
What answer could you give to this?

....

....

....

Worksheet 4

Part 3

Yazid and Alena

1 Do Yazid and Alena interact well with each other? Why/Why not?

....

2 Do they discuss each picture before moving on to the next?

....

3 Do they give reasons for their opinions?

....

4 When she is talking about the photo of the hotel room, Alena says 'It seems too much comfortable than the others rooms.' What would be a more correct sentence?

....

....

5 When he is talking about the photo of the tourists, Yazid says 'Hysterical places also is a good place in the holidays to spend time.' What would be a more a correct sentence?

....

....

6 Do they remember to leave time to make a decision at the end?

....

Worksheet 5

Part 4

Maximiliane and Maxim

1 Who is asked the following questions, Maximiliane, Maxim, or both of them?

   a How important do you think it is to relax and find time to take a holiday? ....

   b What do you think makes a holiday successful? ....

   c Some people think that family hoidays are very stressful. Why do you think this is? ....

   d How important do you think it is to find time to relax and take a holiday? ....

   e Apart from holidays, what other things are necessary for a good life? ....

2 What answers would you give to the questions in 1?

3 Do Maximiliane and Maxim give full answers to their questions?

   ....

4 How many examples does Maximiliane give for what makes a holiday successful?

   ....

5 What does the Interlocutor say at the end of Part 4?

   ....

Giving a good performance

Part 1

Tips

- Be natural.
- Answer as fully as you can.

> **Useful phrases**
>
> I need to think for a moment.
> That's an interesting question.
> Well, it's difficult to say, really.
> Let me see.
> It depends what you mean, exactly.
> I guess the honest answer would be ...
> I suppose the simplest answer to that question is ...
> If I think about it, I suppose ...
> It's hard to generalise, but on balance ...
> The best example that comes to mind is ...

Part 2

Tips

- Speak for a full minute.
- Compare the pictures.
- Answer the question.

> **Useful phrases**
>
> In the first photo ... but in the second one ...
> This picture ... while on the other hand this one ...
> In comparison to the first photo, this one ...

Part 3

Tips

- Discuss each picture in depth.
- Interact with each other.
- Don't reach a decision too soon.

> **Useful phrases**
>
> Let's talk about ... first.
> We could start by talking about ...
> I think we need to make a decision.
> Shall we try to come to an agreement?

Part 4

Tips

- Listen to the question.
- Ask for repetition if necessary.
- Give a full, confident answer.

> **Useful phrases**
>
> Yes, I agree (with you).
> I couldn't agree more.
> So do I./Neither do I.
> That's right/true.
> I see what you mean, but ...
> That may be true, but ...
> Don't you think that ... ?
> That's a good point, but I still think ...

Examiner's questions

Part 1

- Where are you from?

- What do you like about living here/in your country?

- Tell me about your family.

- Do you find it easy to study where you live?

- Is there anything new you'd really like to learn about?

- Who in your family do you spend most time with?

- What job would you really like to do in the future?

Part 2

In this part of the test I'm going to give each of you two photographs. I'd like you to talk about your pictures on your own for about a minute, and also to answer a short question about your partner's photographs.

1 Here are your photographs. They show people spending an afternoon out in different ways. I'd like you to compare the photographs and say what you think the people are enjoying about spending time in these different ways.

   Do you enjoy cycling?

2 Here are your photographs. They show children learning in different ways. I'd like you to compare the photographs and say what you think are the advantages and disadvantages of learning in these different ways.

   What do you think is the best way for children to learn?

Part 3

I'd like you to talk about something together for about three minutes. Here are some pictures showing different things which are important for families when they're on holiday. First, talk to each other about why these things might be important for families when they're on holiday. Then decide which two are most important for a successful family holiday.

Part 4

- How important do you think it is to find time to relax and take a holiday?

- What do you think makes a holiday successful?

Some people think that family holidays are very stressful. Why do you think this is?

Apart from holidays, what other things are necessary for a good life?

How important is it for families to spend time together?

- What are the people enjoying about spending time in these ways?

- What are the advantages and disadvantages of children learning in these ways?

FCE Result

Part 2

- Why might these things be important for families on holiday?
- Which two are most important for a successful family holiday?

FCE Result

Photocopiable © Oxford University Press

Part 3

Answer key

Worksheet 1 page 21

1 two
2 pair
3 global
4 14
5 thank, attending
6 personal life
7 turn
8 minute
9 two
10 compare
11 the (picture) sheet
12 three
13 seven
14 questions
15 Part 3
16 opinion

Worksheet 2 page 22

1 He asks what their names are.
2 a their marksheets
  b He gives them to the Assessor.
3 Yes
4 She mentions all of them.
5 Yes

Worksheet 3 page 23

1 She explains exactly what the task is.
2 No, she gives them to them one at a time (starting with Melanie).
3 No, she starts talking immediately.
4 Yes, she doesn't waste time and so makes the most of the minute available.
5 Yes
6 Yes, she talks until the Interlocutor stops her.
7 Melanie's answer is better because it's longer – Costanza's is quite short and grammatically inaccurate. (She says 'Not a lot, I don't like very much the bike.')
8 Possible answers: Yes I do, because I enjoy taking exercise out in the fresh air/it's a convenient way of getting from one place to another./No I don't because it's quite dangerous cycling where I live because there's a lot of traffic on the roads.

Worksheet 4 page 24

1 Yes, they talk to each other and listen to what each other says and respond well.
2 In most cases yes.
3 Yes
4 Possible answer: 'It seems much more comfortable than (a lot of) other rooms.'
5 Possible answer: 'Historic places/ sites are also somewhere good/a good place to spend time on holiday.'
6 Yes

Worksheet 5 page 25

1 a Maxim
  b Maximiliane
  c both
  d both
  e both
3 Yes
4 three (friends, friendly people, not too many tourists)
5 He says 'Thank you. That's the end of the test.'

Giving a good performance

Part 1 Alena

Alena gives a full answer with reasons and examples.

Part 2 Victoire and Yazid

Victoire spends too much time talking about one photograph and doesn't leave enough time to talk about the second one in any depth.

Yazid moves on to the second photograph too quickly and doesn't talk about either of them in any depth, so he runs out of things to say well before the end of the minute.

Part 3 Maximiliane and Maxim

Maxim initially invites Maximiliane to speak, but they don't then discuss each picture together. Instead they take it in turns to speak about different pictures. They do remember to try to reach a decision at the end.

Part 4 Melanie and Costanza

Both have to be prompted to give more than a very brief answer to their questions.